L is for Last Frontier

An Alaska Alphabet

Written by Carol Crane and Illustrated by Michael Glenn Monroe

Sleeping Bear Press™
310 North Main Street, Suite 300
Chelsea, MI 48118
www.sleepingbearpress.com

© 2007 Sleeping Bear Press is an imprint of The Gale Group, Inc.

Printed and bound in China.

10 9 8 7 6 5

Library of Congress Cataloging-in-Publication Data
Crane, Carol, 1933-
L is for last frontier : an Alaska alphabet / written by Carol Crane ;
illustrated by Michael Glenn Monroe.
p. cm.
Summary: An alphabetical introduction to the state of Alaska.
ISBN: 1-58536-020-1
1. Alaska—Juvenile literature. 2. English language—Alphabet—Juvenile
literature. [1. Alaska. 2. Alphabet.] I. Monroe, Michael Glenn, ill. II. Title.
F904.3 .C73 2002
979.8—dc21   2002003130

There are five distinct groups of Alaska Natives. All have their own beautiful creation stories of their ancestors. These stories are passed on from generation to generation. Their language, cultural beliefs, and the primary regions where they live are all distinct. The five groups are the Northwest Coast Indians, the Inupiaqs-Eskimo, Yupik-Eskimo, Aleut-Alutiq, and the Athabascans.

All of these great people still use each of their inherited hunting skills to subsist on land and sea. For transportation and hunting they use cedar canoes, kayaks, sleds, and snowshoes. However, today more modern vehicles such as snowmobiles are used.

Their clothing is often made of caribou and moose hide. The fur keeps them warm. A mother's fur-lined parka has a large hood for carrying small children. Gloves often have fur on the inside. Moccasins and insulated boots are an important part of their clothing. The sea hunters wear bentwood visors with sea lion whiskers. The number of whiskers shows their success in hunting.

A is for Alaska Natives
remembering their ancestor's way.
Fishing, trapping, hunting, and whaling,
living on a great land today.

Alaska Natives have many artistic skills. Chilkat weavers create perfectly skilled circles. Beautifully carved totem poles are found in Ketchikan and handcrafted Haida cedar canoes, 60 feet long are found here.

Tools are decorated with spiritual symbols to aid in hunting success. Baskets are made that have beautiful geometric designs and are known as the finest in the world. When food is stored for the winter, these great people celebrate using carved wooden masks and elaborate costumes.

Today, some Alaska Natives live and work in the major cities. Some still live off the land as their ancestors once did. In all, these great native people of Alaska will never forget their wonderful heritage.

a

A

Alaska is called bear country because it is the only state to have all three species: The brown bear (or grizzly), the black bear, and the polar bear.

The brown bear has a shoulder hump and a larger head than the black bear. It has large claws for digging, and likes to eat berries, roots, and salmon. A subspecies of the brown bear is the Kodiak bear. It lives exclusively on Kodiak Island and the islands nearby. The Kodiak bear is the largest bear in the world, standing up to 10 feet tall and weighing up to 1,500 pounds.

The black bear has a pointed head and is the smallest of the three bears. It likes to eat berries, honey, fish, and nuts. The black bear and its cubs climb trees to escape from predators.

The polar bear is a carnivore that lives on the Arctic ice pack. Its main diet consists of ringed seals, walrus pups, and stranded whales. It has a heavy white coat, a long neck, and small head. The polar bear uses its webbed front feet like paddles to swim through the water. A cub will hold on to its mother's tail and swim along with her.

Bb

B is for the three Bears,
brown bear, polar, and black.
Mother bear with her cubs,
hunts for a morning snack.

Cranberries are found on high bush, low bush, and bog shrubs throughout Alaska. The red berries are bright and shiny and are used for jellies, relishes, and drinks. The Alaska Natives use the berries for medicine.

Blueberries are sometimes called huckleberries. They are sweet and are used in jams and jellies. The Alaska Natives use them in a dessert called akutuq made of oil, fat, sugar, and blueberries. Where there are blueberries, you may also find bears. Mountain goats, elk, and deer also love to eat the berries.

Crowberries are also called blackberries. Alaska Natives cook them rather than eat them raw. They blend them with livers of cod or trout into a dish called tingaulik.

Soapberry is called the whipped-cream berry. Northwest coast native people whip the red-orange berries to make an Eskimo ice cream.

C is for Cranberries.
People love them, so do bears.
Blueberries, crowberries, soapberries too,
an Alaskan berry fair.

Mountains crowned with snow,
an awesome sight to see.
This one's called "The Great One,"
Denali starts with **D**.

d

D

Denali is the name the Athabascan native people gave the high peaks of Mount McKinley. This wondrous mountain was named for President William McKinley. Mount McKinley is the highest mountain in the North American continent with a summit of 20,320 feet. The high crown of Mount McKinley continues to be a focal point for this great state.

During President Jimmy Carter's term in office, a bill was signed establishing Denali National Park and Preserve. The park area is home to a variety of wildlife and more than 600 species of flowering plants.

E e

The bald eagle is the national symbol of the United States. There are up to 30,000 bald eagles living in Alaska. Eagles are known to live 20 or more years. After these eagles are five years old, the color of their head and tail feathers turn white. Eagles have very sharp eyes and can spot fish in the water a mile away. They have a wide wingspan of over eight feet. By law, eagles are protected from hunters.

Both the bald eagle and the golden eagle are found in Alaska. They are known as birds of prey, which means they feed mainly on the animals they hunt. Other birds of prey are hawks, falcons, and owls.

E is for Eagles,
soaring, looking for food.
Swooping wings, sharp talons,
a salmon for the brood.

The forget-me-not is Alaska's official state flower. It is a delicate little flower that grows along streams and alpine meadows throughout most of Alaska.

In 1926, a 13-year-old Native American boy, Bennie Benson, received 1st prize for his entry in a flag design contest for Alaska. The blue field of the flag represents the sky, sea, and mountain lakes, as well as the wildflowers of Alaska. On the flag are eight gold stars. Seven stars form the constellation the Big Dipper, and the eighth is the North Star representing Alaska, the northernmost state in our country. The flag became the official state flag in 1959.

The four-spot skimmer dragonfly is the official insect of Alaska. It naturally controls the mosquito population because it eats many of these pesky insects.

F

Ff

F is for Forget-Me-Not,
it catches your eye.
F is also for our state flag,
in a bright blue sky.

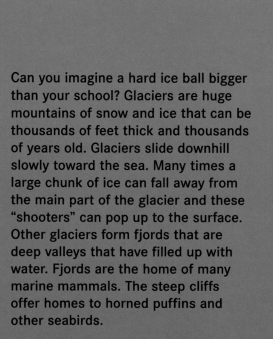

Can you imagine a hard ice ball bigger than your school? Glaciers are huge mountains of snow and ice that can be thousands of feet thick and thousands of years old. Glaciers slide downhill slowly toward the sea. Many times a large chunk of ice can fall away from the main part of the glacier and these "shooters" can pop up to the surface. Other glaciers form fjords that are deep valleys that have filled up with water. Fjords are the home of many marine mammals. The steep cliffs offer homes to horned puffins and other seabirds.

G is for Glaciers,
ice and snow formed in Arctic weather.
Moving ever so slowly,
over many years joined together.

Another name for hooligan is eula-chon (you-la-kon). It is a slim, oily, silvery-blue fish that can grow to be eight inches long. The hooligan lays its eggs in rivers and streams and then returns to live in the ocean. This fish is so oily that it can be used as a candle by sticking a wick into its mouth, then positioning it upright and lighting the wick. Hooligan oil, soapberries, and sugar can be beaten together like whipped cream to make Eskimo ice cream.

H
h

H is for Hooligan,
a slim and oily fish.
These fish have many uses,
even an ice cream dish.

I is for the Iditarod,
from Anchorage to Nome.
Mush my huskies, hurry!
We're almost home.

In 1997, the Iditarod race marked its 25th anniversary. In 1976, Congress designated the more than 1,000-mile trail as a national historic trail. The race crosses two mountains, follows the Yukon River for about 150 miles, runs through several bush villages, and crosses the pack ice of Norton Sound. Originally a mail route blazed in 1910, the Iditarod trail became a legend in 1925 when sled-dog mushers delivered diphtheria serum to Nome to help stop an epidemic.

A sled-dog racer starts with 16 dogs. The team must finish the race with at least five dogs. Since racers are not allowed to replace dogs, fewer dogs remain at the end of the race. The dogs wear booties to protect their feet while running. They eat special food to give them energy and are checked often during the race for injuries. The racers are very caring and tend to the dogs lovingly. Sled-dog racing is Alaska's official state sport.

Juneau is very unique. It is the only capital city in the U.S. that does not have a road leading into it. If you want to go to Juneau, you either take a ferryboat or an airplane. The Alaska Marine Highway is a very important ferryboat transportation system.

Juneau was built on the Gastineau Channel and backs up to Mt. Juneau. Around 1880, Joe Juneau and Richard Harris found pebble-sized gold nuggets in this area's creek beds and mountain terrain. The city was named after Joe Juneau, the first gold prospector to come to this region.

Jade is Alaska's state gem. It is mined and used for jewelry, bookends, clock faces, and tabletops. Most of Alaska's jade is found north of the Arctic Circle.

J j

J is for Juneau, our capital,
a city so near yet so far.
Travel there by plane or boat,
but you can't get there by car.

K k

K is for King Salmon,
Alaska's official state fish.
A true king in size,
to hook one is a fisherman's wish.

The salmon lays its eggs in rivers, streams, and lakes. After traveling up to five years and hundreds of miles in the ocean, the salmon returns to its original birthplace. Scientists still consider it a great mystery that the salmon can find the exact river or stream where it was hatched.

The salmon is a major source of food for both the animals and people of Alaska. Bears, eagles, wolves, and other animals easily hunt salmon when the fish swim in large numbers to spawn.

L1

Loons have haunting laughs and wails that can be heard throughout the Alaskan woods. There are five different species of loons in the world and they can be found in Alaska's ponds, rivers, and lakes. The five species are the common, yellow-billed, red-throated, pacific, and arctic loons. Loons build their nests close to the water's edge. They are often seen swimming with their babies on their backs. Loons are known as the "spirit of the wilderness."

L is also for the Last Frontier in America. In Alaska, old customs and modern ways exist together. Today, you can see mountains, rainforests, tundra, rugged islands, and glaciers that were seen by the original native people. It is with awe and respect we view this wild, beautiful land.

L is for Loon,
hear it coo and cry,
nesting with its babies,
singing loon lullabies.

M is for Moose,
antlers big as a king's crown.
Lives in the woods but
often found in any town.

Moose are members of the deer family. The male moose have magnificent antlers, but they can be very dangerous. During mating season, moose have been known to charge people, cars, dogs, and trains. Moose weigh up to 1,600 pounds. Mosquitoes and other insects bite moose, but they submerge themselves in water to get away from the pesky bugs. Moose eat a variety of water plants, willow, birch, and aspen twigs. Calves can weigh up to 600 pounds by the age of one.

Other members of the deer family found in Alaska are the Sitka black-tailed deer, the Roosevelt elk, the caribou, and the reindeer.

m

M

N n

N is for the Northern Lights,
    mysterious colored glow.
Sweeping across the sky,
    a shimmering night time show.

"Thar she blows!" we cry out in delight,
seeing the water spout blow.
Black and white with tall dorsal fin,
the Orca whale is our O.

An orca is called a killer whale because it attacks other whales, seals, and sea lions. The killer whale is really a member of the dolphin family. It can weigh up to 10 tons. A group of whales is called a pod and may include up to 40 whales in each pod. An orca's call is distinctive enough that each family member can recognize it. You can identify an orca whale by its tall dorsal fin which has white and black markings.

The humpback whale is seen most frequently along the southern coast of Alaska. A newborn humpback whale weighs 4,000 pounds and is 12 feet long.

The bowhead whale is the official ocean mammal of Alaska. It is the only whale that spends its entire life near sea ice and does not travel to warm waters to have its babies.

O o

P p

The willow ptarmigan looks like a small grouse. It eats willow twigs and birch bark in winter, and berries, insects, seeds, and buds in the summer. This bird has water repellent inner and outer feathers. It even has feathers on the soles of its feet, which help it walk on snow. The ptarmigan takes flight and then dives into the snow for warmth and protection. Because it flies into the snow instead of walking, the ptarmigan does not leave a track that predators can spot. Once inside its snow home, the ptarmigan is warm and safe. This bird is very brave to live all year in the Arctic where it could become a meal for a hungry animal.

P is for the Ptarmigan,
    with feathers on the soles of its feet.
This is Alaska's state bird,
    walking easily on snow and sleet.

The musk ox of Alaska is never cold. It can brave below zero temperatures very easily because of its long over-coat of underhair. This soft underhair is called qiviut. The musk ox produces up to seven pounds of qiviut each year. Alaska Natives collect qiviut from the ground and bushes after it has fallen off the ox. The underhair is gathered and knit into caps and scarves in a variety of patterns.

The musk ox looks the same as its ancestors did 100,000 years ago. Its fur is parted down the middle of its head, and it has curved horns on both sides. Adult oxen form a circle around their young to protect them from their enemy, the wolf.

Q is for Qiviut,
　　musk oxen's long underhair.
Knit into scarves and hats,
　　warm and soft for winter wear.

R r

The Alaska rainforest is made up of the Chugach and the Tongass National Forests. These ancient forests have giant trees hundreds of feet tall and almost 1,000 years old. It is the home of the brown bear and hundreds of bald eagles. The forest is also the home of river otters, deer, wolves, mountain goats, and salmon that return to spawn. The rainforest becomes endangered when people cut down too many trees. Very little wildlife and vegetation can grow in these clear cuts.

Rainforest starts with R,
   beautiful, remote, and green.
A gift for the world,
   an untouched earth that's clean.

The Sitka spruce only grows in Alaska's southeast coastal rainforests. This tree looks like a tall church steeple and is over 1,000 years old. The Northwest coast folk regard this dark green tree as sacred and use its bark, roots, and boughs in many ways. The boughs make soft beds to lie on, the lumber is used to build boats, and the roots are made into baskets and nets. The sap from the tree provides a healing balm for cuts.

S is for Sitka Spruce,
official tree of our state.
Growing up two-hundred feet,
so tall and very straight!

T is for Tundra,
a treeless arctic plain.
Short warm summers,
in winter, a frozen terrain.

The tundra is a huge dinner table for animals and insects in the summer. With constant sunshine in the summer months, food becomes plentiful, and animals raise their young and store meals for the upcoming winter. Millions of birds migrate to the tundra to feast, make nests, and hatch their eggs. Mosquitoes and other insects lay their eggs in ponds and lakes.

In the winter, plants shelter themselves from the arctic cold by growing low to the ground. For those animals that stay on the tundra during the winter, digging through the snow to find food is difficult. There is little sunlight and many animals hibernate to avoid the cold. Plants and insects become dormant. The tundra has been called Alaska's cold desert.

T t

U is for Umiak,
open skin covered boat.
Used by the Eskimos for whaling,
easy for one to tote.

The umiak is made from walrus hide that is stretched over a wooden frame. The boat can be 35 to 40 feet in length. The hide is very strong and can withstand sharp sea ice. This boat can skim along the water very quietly and is still used today to hunt whales, seals, and walrus.

Umiaks are so lightweight that hunters can walk them out onto the ice. They can then put them into the open water.

U
u

V is for Alaska Vegetables,
just look at their monster size!
Broccoli, cabbage, pumpkins, and more,
Alaska State Fair's first prize.

5 · · · · 10 · · · · 15 · · · · 20 · · · · 25 · · · · 30 · · · · 35 · · · · 40 · · · · · 45

There are only fourteen weeks of good growing weather in Alaska. Plants grow rapidly though, because of the long days and abundant sunlight and rainfall. Enormous vegetables are brought to the state fair each year. The current record holders are: broccoli, 39 1/2 pounds; cabbage, 98 pounds; celery, 25 pounds; mushroom, 25 pounds; pumpkin, 196 pounds; and squash, 303 pounds. How many people would this huge squash feed?

Alaska is known as the Land of the Midnight Sun. From mid-November until late January the sun does not rise in Barrow, Alaska. Barrow is the northernmost town in Alaska. When the sunshine finally rises, everyone celebrates with songs. Then Barrow enjoys 84 days of continuous sunlight. At midnight, there is still sunlight and the children may not want to go to bed.

Wolves run in packs of up to 30 members. They can run miles at a time looking for food to feed their family. They are found in almost all areas of Alaska. Some are gray or black while others vary in colors ranging from brown or tan to white. Most wolves howl to talk to other members of their family. Maybe they are asking, "Where are you?" Wolves have litters of 3 to 10 pups. Pups are born deaf and blind. They stay close to the den until they are three weeks old. The mother wolf stays with her pups while other members of the pack go looking for food.

W is for the Arctic Wolves,
white phantoms in the snow.
Looking, sniffing for each meal,
feet quiet as a shadow.

When the news came that gold had been discovered in Alaska, men left their jobs, homes, and families to head west. Not all struck it rich though because many could not endure the hard life of traveling and the cold weather. Gold was first discovered in 1848. Three of the largest nuggets were found near Nome. Staking a claim entitled a man to pan for gold, which meant swirling rocks and water in a screened pan until specks or nuggets would appear. Another way to mine for gold was by using a pick and shovel to dig in the side of a mountain.

Gold was adopted as Alaska's state mineral in 1968.

X

X

Now, X marks the spot for gold,
searching every mountain and stream.

And Y is for the Yukon River,
that held every gold digger's dream.

Y y

The Yukon River is the longest river in Alaska and the third longest in the United States. Prospectors used the river for boat travel in the summer and as a sled trail to follow in the winter. It was the dream of every man who set out for Alaska to find gold, and indeed, the Yukon River Basin was one of three locations where this precious metal was found.

Z z

Arctic Ocean

Walrus

Bald Eagle

Snow Goose

Z is for Zoodles of wildlife,
Arctic nature, untamed and free.
Birds, bears, and bowhead whales,
how many animals do you see?

Bowhead Whale

Tundra Swan

Alaska's assortment of wildlife is unmatched by any other state. Walrus, musk oxen, and polar bears represent just a few of the animals that live only in this Arctic wonderland. From nearly 300 species of birds to more than 400 kinds of fish and 105 types of mammals, let's discover Alaska's diverse animal kingdom.

Polar Bear

Wolverine

Mountain Goat

Canada

Alaska

Lynx

Snowshoe Hare

Alaska has so much to see.
It's America's largest state.
So let's go back to letter A,
and read how it's truly great.

Ptarmigan

Brown Bear

King Salmon

Gulf of Alaska

Steller's Sea Lion

Orca Whale

Pacific Ocean

A Frontier Full of Facts

1. How many miles long is the Iditarod race?
2. What capital city in Alaska can only be reached by boat or airplane?
3. Alaska is the only state to have all three species of bears. What are the three species?
4. Why are eagles called birds of prey?
5. If you wanted to make Eskimo ice cream, what three ingredients would you use?
6. What do Alaska's natives do with qiviut?
7. Enormous vegetables are entered in Alaska's State Fair. What is the current record weight for a pumpkin?
8. What animal pup is born deaf and blind?
9. How high is Mount McKinley?
10. What fish can travel up to five years and still remember how to come back to where it was born?

1. The Iditarod race is over 1,000 miles long.
2. Juneau can only be reached by only boat or airplane.
3. The black bear, brown bear, and polar bear are the three species of bears that live in Alaska.
4. Eagles are called birds of prey because they feed mainly on the animals that they hunt.
5. Eskimo ice cream contains three ingredients: hooligan oil, soapberries, and sugar.
6. Qiviut is gathered from the ground and knit into caps and scarves.
7. The current record for the largest pumpkin entered in the fair is 196 pounds.
8. Arctic wolves are born deaf and blind.
9. Mount McKinley is 20,320 feet high.
10. The king salmon can travel up to five years and hundreds of miles in the ocean and return to its original birthplace.

Carol Crane

Carol Crane has worked for 25 years reviewing, lecturing, and enjoying children's literature. As a respected national educational consultant, she travels extensively and speaks at state reading conventions across the United States.

Carol has opened up a new page in writing children's books that are fun to read as well as useful in the classroom. She is the author of *S is for Sunshine: A Florida Alphabet* as well as its companion title, *Sunny Numbers: A Florida Counting Book*. She also authored *L is for Lone Star: A Texas Alphabet*. Carol lives with her husband Conrad in Bradenton, Florida.

Michael Glenn Monroe

Renowned wildlife artist Michael Glenn Monroe has been selected to paint the 2002 National Easter Egg. He is also the winner of the 1997 Michigan Duck Stamp award. Michael visits schools and teaches children simple shapes and techniques they can use to begin drawing.

He has illustrated many children's books including *Buzzy the bumblebee*; *M is for Mitten: A Michigan Alphabet*; *S is for Sunshine: A Florida Alphabet Book*; *The Michigan Counting Book*; *A Wish To Be A Christmas Tree*; and *Foursome the Spider*.

Michael lives in Brighton, Michigan with his wife Colleen, and children, Matthew, Natalie, and John.

Reference List

Alaska Rain Forest Campaign [Online].
http://www.akrain.org/rainforest/landpeople.asp
[Accessed 2002].

Barrett, Pam. 1998. *Insight Guide Alaska.*
APA Publications.

Calef, George. 1981. *Caribou and the Barren-lands.*
Firefly Books.

Ewing, Susan. 1996. *The Great Alaska Nature
Factbook.* Alaska Northwest.

Markle, Sandra. 2000. *Growing up Wild with Bears.*
Atheneum.

Mace, Alice. 1998. *The Birds Around Us.*
Ortho Books.

McQuiston, Schmidt & Thom. 1994.
*In the Spirit of Mother Earth: Nature in Native
American Art.* Chronicle.

Milepost Ed.1997. *Alaska A to Z.* Vernon
Publications.

Sydeman, Michelle & Lund, Annabel. 1996.
Alaska Wildlife Viewing Guide. Falcon Publishing.

Wuerthner, George. 1995. *Beautiful America's
Alaska.* Beautiful America Publishing Company.